WORLD WAR ONE
HISTORY IN AN HOUR

Also in the *History in an Hour* series

1066
The Afghan Wars
The American Civil War
American Slavery
Ancient Egypt
Black History
The Cold War
Dickens
George Washington
The Gunpowder Plot
Henry VIII's Wives
Hitler
JFK
The Medieval Anarchy
Nazi Germany
The Queen
The Reformation
The Russian Revolution
The Siege of Leningrad
South Africa
Stalin
Titanic
The Vietnam War
World War Two

World War One

History in an Hour

RUPERT COLLEY

WILLIAM
COLLINS

William Collins
An imprint of HarperCollins*Publishers* Ltd
77–85 Fulham Palace Road
Hammersmith, London W6 8JB
www.harpercollins.co.uk

Visit the History in an Hour website:
www.historyinanhour.com

Published by William Collins in 2013

First published as an eBook by Harper*Press* in 2012

A catalogue record for this book
is available from the British Library

ISBN 978-0-00-753911-6

Set in Minion by FMG using Atomik ePublisher from Easypress

Contents

Introduction   1

Assassination of an Archduke   3
The Schlieffen Plan   7
The Eastern Front   11
Global War   13
The War in Britain   15
The Western Front   19
Gallipoli   23
The Ottoman Empire   27
Verdun   29
Trenches   31
Change at the Top   35
Air and Sea   39
Ireland and Easter Monday   41
Russia and Revolution   43
USA   47
Passchendaele   49
The Spring Offensive, 1918   51
The Hundred Days   53
Armistice   57
Paris Peace Conference   59
The War to End War?   61

Appendix One: Key Players   63
Appendix Two: Timeline of World War One   81

Introduction

The 'Great War', as it was originally called, lasted 1,568 days from 28 July 1914 to 11 November 1918, and was without parallel. It brought to an end four dynasties, ignited revolution, and forged new nations. Modern warfare introduced killing on an unprecedented scale, costing an estimated nine million lives. This was a war of new technology and terrifying new weapons. It was the war that killed the idealistic notion of battle – a war without chivalry, romance or glory – a war that shattered mind and body.

This, the first 'world' war, was not just about armies winning and losing battles, but whole populations mobilized for war, at the mercy of the enemy, civilians starved and bombed. It was an industrial war where a country's whole economic output was geared to war; a war of empires that pulled in combatants from nations across the globe. It was a war of land, air and sea, a war of politics, espionage, and also the Home Front. For the first time in history, this was total war.

And this, in an hour, is World War One.

Assassination of an Archduke

It all began with two deaths.

On Sunday, 28 June 1914, the heir to the Austrian-Hungarian (Habsburg) throne, the Archduke Franz Ferdinand and his wife, the Countess Sophie, paid an official visit to Sarajevo, capital of Bosnia, to inspect troops of the Austrian-Hungarian army.

Bosnia had been a recent and unwilling addition to the Habsburg Empire. Resentful Bosnian Serbs dreamt of freedom and incorporation into the nation of Serbia. Nationalistic groups formed, determined to use violence to strike terror at the heart of the Austrian-Hungarian empire. One such group, the sinisterly named 'Black Hand', included among its number a nineteen-year-old named Gavrilo Princip. It was in Sarajevo that Princip would change the world.

Princip and a handful of his Black Hand comrades arrived,

each armed with a bomb and, in the event of failure, a vial of cyanide. They joined, at various intervals, the throng of onlookers lining a six-kilometre route and waited for the six-car motorcade to come into view. The first two would-be assassins lost their nerve, while the third managed to throw his bomb, causing injury to a driver but leaving the Archduke and his wife unharmed. Racked with a sense of failure, Princip trudged to a nearby tavern.

The Archduke, having delivered a speech, decided to visit the wounded driver in hospital. On his way, his driver took a wrong turning down a one-way street, a street named after Franz Ferdinand's uncle, the emperor, Franz Joseph, along which was a tavern. Princip, astonished to see the royal car, acted on impulse. Jumping onto the running board as the driver tried to engage the reverse gear, he fired two shots. Mortally wounded, Franz Ferdinand's last words were: 'Sophie, stay alive for the children.' It was not to be. The Archduke and his wife died together. It was their fourteenth wedding anniversary.

The Road to War

The assassination of Franz Ferdinand had very much been the work of Princip and his band of Black Hand conspirators but the Austrian-Hungarian empire saw an opportunity to assert its authority over Serbia. First it sought reassurance from its powerful ally, Germany. Together, they had formed the Dual Alliance in 1879 which, three years later, became the Triple Alliance when Italy added its signature. Now, the German Kaiser, Wilhelm II, gave Austria-Hungary the assurance it needed, then promptly went off on a cruise around Norway.

It took the Austrian-Hungarian government three weeks but the ultimatum they sent Serbia was, in the words of Britain's foreign secretary, Sir Edward Grey, the 'most formidable document ever sent from one nation to another'. Serbia was given forty-eight hours to comply with ten demands, specifically designed to humiliate and therefore be rejected. Although the Serbs agreed to eight, it was never going to be enough for the bellicose Austrian-Hungarians and on 28 July they declared war on Serbia.

Events now moved quickly, one triggering off another. In response to this declaration of war, Russia, which saw itself as protector of Serbia, began to mobilize. France, Russia's ally since 1892, offered her its support. In response, the Germans gave Russia twelve hours to halt its mobilization. The deadline passed, thus on 1 August, Germany declared war on Russia and, two days later, on France. 'The sword has been forced into our hand,' claimed the Kaiser.

The Schlieffen Plan

Germany now faced a war on both its western and eastern borders; a war on two fronts. But it was a prospect they had long anticipated. In 1905, the then Chief of Staff, Count Alfred von Schlieffen, had devised a plan for such an eventuality. Russia, he surmised, not incorrectly, would take up to six weeks to mobilize its armies, allowing Germany time to defeat France. In order to avoid the line of fortifications on the Franco-German border, the German army would have to advance through neutral Belgium in a huge sweeping movement: 'Let the last man on the right brush the Channel with his sleeve.' Having knocked out Belgium, it would swing south, covering twenty kilometres a day, and encircle Paris. Having dealt with the French, it would then have time to move east to confront the vast armies of Russia. Schlieffen died in 1913. One year later, his grand plan was put into action.

Speed was of the essence. On 2 August, Germany stormed

through Luxembourg and demanded immediate access through Belgium. But 'Poor little Belgium', as the British press called her, refused and turned to an 1839 treaty, guaranteeing its neutrality. One of the signatories was Germany. The other was Great Britain. Britain asked Germany for an assurance that they would respect Belgium's neutrality. Germany ignored it and on 4 August began bombing the city of Liège. Germany could not believe that Britain would go to war with a 'kindred nation' over a 'scrap of paper' – a treaty signed seventy-five years before. Britain declared war on Germany on 4 August. Sir Edward Grey, gazing out from the Foreign Office, remarked, 'The lamps are going out all over Europe. We shall not see them lit again in our lifetime.'

Grey, in his gloominess, was in a minority – the rest of Europe rejoiced at the prospect of war. Everywhere, civilians gathered in town squares to celebrate, young men anticipated adventures of derring-do and chivalry. 'It'll all be over by Christmas,' the British army was told; 'You'll be home before the leaves fall,' declared the Kaiser to his troops. For the Russian Tsar, Nicholas II, a victorious war would stifle the murmurings of revolution that were infecting his kingdom. For France, still chafing over its defeat in the Franco–Prussian War in 1871, war offered a chance to re-establish its reputation.

Unlike her European counterparts, Britain had no standing army, only a small professional force, the British Expeditionary Force (BEF), numbering a mere 100,000 men (compared, for example, to Germany's 1.1 million). It was this tiny army that arrived in northern France to bolster the French effort. The Kaiser dismissed the BEF as a 'contemptible little army', hence British soldiers took pride in calling themselves the 'Old Contemptibles'.

The first major confrontation between the Great Powers took place in the Belgian town of Mons on 23 August; Britain's first battle on mainland Europe since Waterloo almost a century before. The 'contemptible' BEF, despite being outnumbered three to one, inflicted huge casualties on the Germans, delayed their advance, and then retreated in good order. The Retreat from Mons was, as legend would have it, guided by the 'Angels of Mons', ghostly apparitions who safely led the British soldiers away from the battlefield.

The Germans advanced through France but were rapidly running out of steam, too exhausted to maintain the momentum. By early September they had reached the River Marne, only thirty miles north of Paris. The military commander of Paris, General Joseph Gallieni, was old enough to remember 1871 when the Prussians, Germany's predecessors, had besieged the capital to the point of starvation. He had no intention of allowing the Germans anywhere near Paris again.

After three days of fighting at the Marne, the Germans looked poised to break through the French and British forces, and on to Paris. Gallieni was to send reinforcements but while he had the troops he had no means to transport them north. In a flash of ingenuity, he seized every available Parisian taxi – 600 of them – crammed each one full of soldiers and sent them on their way to meet the army of the French commander-in-chief, General Joseph Joffre.

The arrival of Gallieni's taxis saved the day. It was on the River Marne that the Schlieffen Plan came to a shuddering halt. Paris was safe and now it was the turn of the Germans to retreat. They fell back, forty miles north, to the River Aisne where they stopped and dug in. The Allies tried to dislodge the Germans from their defensive positions but, failing to do so, began to dig their own trenches.

General Joffre moved part of his force northwards of the Aisne to try and outflank the Germans. The Germans, now led by Erich von Falkenhayn, moved a comparable number of men to block Joffre's manoeuvre. Joffre repeated his tactic – as did the Germans, each side constructing trenches as it went along. It developed into what became known as the 'Race to the Sea' as each army tried to outlap the other until they both hit the Channel. A similar charade extended the line of trenches south from the Aisne to the Swiss border.

The war of movement had come to an end. The consolidation of defence had triumphed over attack. Stretching 400 miles from the English Channel to Switzerland lay a network of trenches. They were to remain, by and large, in place for four long years. As 1914 drew to a close, the idea of a short, sharp war had all but vanished. Offence was no match for deeply entrenched defence. Generals on all sides puzzled over this uncomfortable truth.

On Christmas Day, 1914, British troops in the front-line trenches could hear the Germans singing 'Stille Nacht' (Silent Night). The British joined in. Cautiously, soldiers on both sides climbed out of their trenches and walked towards each other across No Man's Land. They shook hands, exchanged cigarettes, and took photographs of each other. Further up the line, a group of Scots played the Germans at football with helmets for goalposts. The Germans won 3–2. But the festivities had to end. With reluctant handshakes, they each returned to their trenches and grudgingly took up their arms. This fraternization was very much against orders. It was never to happen to such a large extent again.

The Eastern Front

War had begun on the Eastern Front. Two Russian armies bore down into East Prussia, while the German army was led by the formidable duo of Generals Paul von Hindenburg and Erich Ludendorff. The Germans, in full possession of Russian plans, decimated the first Russian army. 'The tsar trusted me,' wailed the Russian commander, Alexander Samsonov. 'How can I ever face him again?' He didn't – he walked into a nearby wood and shot himself. The second Russian army fared no better. The Battles of Tannenberg and the Masurian Lakes went down as terrible defeats for Russia. The Austrian-Hungarian empire, the instigators of this whole war, was faring no better.

The Germans now found themselves in the very situation they had wanted to avoid – a war on two fronts. A system of over 1,000 miles of defensive trenches appeared on the Eastern Front. Unlike the Western Front, the front lines in the east were often as much as fifty miles apart, were not continuous, and were lightly defended. German sources of manpower and equipment were stretched even further when, throughout the war, they were obliged to send reinforcements to help the Austrian-Hungarians. They felt as if they were 'shackled to a corpse'.

Global War

The British asked their dominions to seize nearby German colonies, requests that were gladly accepted. By October 1914, Samoa had fallen to New Zealand, and German New Guinea and the Bismarck Archipelago (modern-day Papua New Guinea) to Australia.

Japan declared war on Germany on 23 August 1914 and promptly seized all the German-held islands in the North Pacific. In September, Japanese forces landed in neutral China and laid siege to the German base at Tsingtao on the coast of China, capturing it on 7 November.

In Africa, the war was fought against the German colonies. In German East Africa, the maverick German commander, Paul von Lettow-Vorbeck, held out for the whole war, only surrendering on 23 November 1918. Elsewhere, Germany lost its colonies in West Africa with Togoland and Cameroon falling to the Allies, and in the south where South Africa conquered German South West Africa (Namibia) with relative ease.

On 23 May 1915, Italy entered the war on the side of the Allies. Having joined the Triple Alliance with Germany and Austria–Hungary in 1882, Italy had kept its neutrality until lured into war on the Allies' side by British promises of Habsburg territory.

The War in Britain

Britain had a problem with men – not enough of them. The BEF, the professional army, was too small but the British, unlike their European counterparts, were against conscription. The answer was to raise an army of volunteers. The Secretary of State for War, Field Marshal Lord Horatio Kitchener, went on a recruitment drive. Throughout the country from 7 August 1914, posters adorned with his stern-looking face and pointing finger shouted out, 'Your Country Needs You.'

Kitchener and the government hoped for perhaps 100,000 volunteers within the first six months. Any more would cause logistical problems. In the event, they got two million by the end of 1915, such was the extent of British patriotism and British naivety. But these young men were not to blame for their ignorance – news reporting was severely censored and war reporters were barred from the front. Thus, speculation and rumour made up for a lack of facts. A million Russian troops had landed in Scotland and were marching through England – you could see the snow on their boots; the barbaric Germans had tied Belgian nuns to church bells and used them as clappers; and the corpses of German soldiers were being used by the Germans to make candles and boot polish.

While men signed up, women took their jobs in factories, on farms, in public transport, postal services, and businesses. The war, arguably, advanced the cause of women's liberation far more than the pre-war suffragette movement. Recognizing the role women played during the war, the British government passed two laws in 1918 that, between them, gave women over thirty the right to vote, and allowed women to stand as Members of Parliament.

On 27 January 1916, the recruiting of volunteers in Britain came to an end, replaced by conscription. Initially affecting only single men, by May the draft was extended to include married men.

The growing disillusionment with war is perhaps best reflected in the works of the War Poets. At first, poems extolled the glory of war and the virtues of defending one's country. Rupert Brooke epitomized the early enthusiasm for war in his sonnet 'Now God be thanked who has matched us with His hour'. Julian Grenfell, a captain in the British army, wrote in a letter, 'I adore war. It is like a big picnic but without the objectivelessness of a picnic.' His poem, 'Into Battle', in which he wrote of the 'joy of battle', was published in *The Times* on the day of his funeral in May 1915.

Bitterness soon crept in. Siegfried Sassoon, an early enthusiast for the war, had received the Military Cross and was nicknamed Mad Jack for his courageous feats. While recovering from shell shock in Craiglockhart hospital in Scotland, Sassoon wrote of the 'rank stench of those bodies [that] haunts me still'. Sassoon befriended a fellow patient, Wilfred Owen, who summed up his generation's disillusionment with war in his poem, 'Dulce et Decorum est': 'You would not tell with such high zest to children ardent for some desperate glory, / The old Lie: *Dulce et Decorum est / Pro patria mori*' ('it is sweet and right to die for your country'). Owen was killed in action a week before the Armistice.

Spies, according to the fevered public imagination, were everywhere – you could spot German spies dressed as nuns by their hairy legs. Genuine Germans were interned on the Isle of Man. Anti-German sentiment ran deep – shops with Germanic-sounding names were attacked, dachshunds, according to popular legend, kicked in the street. Even the Royal Family was not immune, changing its name from Saxe-Coburg-Gotha, a bit of a German giveaway, to Windsor.

In Belgium, English nurse Edith Cavell was caught smuggling wounded Allied soldiers into neutral Netherlands. Despite appeals for clemency, Cavell was executed on 12 October 1915 by firing squad. Cavell had freely admitted her guilt for a crime that carried the death penalty, but the British government seized on the propaganda advantage Cavell's death provided – the heroic nurse murdered by the German barbarian. Another infamous execution was that of Gertrud Margarete Zelle, an exotic Dutch dancer and performer better known by her stage name, Mata Hari. Accused by the French of being a double agent, she was shot in October 1917.

Hatred of all things German intensified when, on 19 January 1915, German zeppelins bombed Great Yarmouth in East Anglia, killing four people. The first raid on London, on 31 May, killed seven. War had come to England. Compared with the next war, these attacks were few and infrequent, and the damage limited. In total, 557 British civilians lost their lives from bombing throughout the war.

More shocking perhaps was the sinking of the British Cunard cruise liner, the *Lusitania*, off the coast of County Cork, Ireland. Hit by a German U-boat on 7 May 1915, the ship sank in just eighteen minutes. Of its 1,959 passengers and crew 1,198 were killed, 128 of whom were American. The attack on a civilian ship caused outrage but the ship had been carrying a large supply of ammunition, which therefore, in German eyes, made her a legitimate target.

The Western Front

The attrition on both fronts continued with varying degrees of success and failure; any success being usually short-lived and ultimately inconsequential, yet still costly in terms of lives.

On 22 April 1915, during the Second Battle of Ypres, the Germans introduced a new element to the Western Front – at 5 p.m. a yellowy vapour smelling of chlorine floated over the French lines. It was gas – 5,730 cylinders of it. French and Algerian soldiers, retching and panicked, ran off, leaving a four-mile gap for the Germans to attack unimpeded. However, the Germans, wary of stepping into the cloud protected only by their crude gas masks, felt unable to exploit the opportunity. This new terrible weapon was inhumane, cried the Allied generals, only to be using it themselves within five months.

Gas had been used three months before on the Eastern Front but in the freezing temperatures the chemicals froze and failed to vaporize. Having experimented with chlorine, Fritz Haber, pioneer of gas warfare, developed a new, more effective gas, called phosgene, which emitted a smell akin to freshly cut grass. Its first use, again on the Eastern Front, in January 1916, proved successful. Haber and his associates celebrated. Haber's wife, appalled by her husband's barbarous innovation, took his service revolver and shot herself.

In 1917, the Germans introduced mustard gas, so named because of its odour, which could penetrate clothing and be absorbed through skin. Gas had become a common feature by the end of the war. Although it was effective at incapacitating troops and causing long-term illness, gas accounted for only 3 per cent of fatalities. Another German invention, the flamethrower, was introduced into battle against the French in February 1915. But it was the artillery that caused by far the most damage throughout the war.

Following Kitchener's recruitment drive, the British army now had the men but not the crucial equipment: weapons, ammunition, clothing, and even accommodation were all lacking. Following British failure at the Battle of Aubers Bridge in May 1915, the British commander-in-chief, Sir John French, leaked the want of ammunition to *The Times*, which picked up the story, blaming the Liberal government of Lord Asquith. Politically, the 'Shell Scandal' proved fatal. The Liberal government was forced into a coalition with the Conservatives. Herbert Asquith remained prime minister, but, weakened, he survived for only another nineteen months.

In September 1915, at the Battle of Loos, Britain first used gas – 140 tons. But the wind made a mockery of General Douglas Haig's plans, and over 2,000 British soldiers suffered as the gas floated back towards their lines, although only seven died as a consequence. After a month of futile attack at the cost of some 50,000 British lives, the offensive was called off, finishing on 14

October. Haig may have been commander in the field, but it was Sir John French, as commander-in-chief, who fell. In December French was replaced by Haig.

Gallipoli

In October 1914, Turkey (the Ottoman Empire) entered the war on the side of the Central Powers and on Christmas Day went on the offensive against the Russians, launching an attack through the Caucasus. The Tsar sent an appeal to Britain, asking for a diversionary attack that would ease the pressure on Russia. In the event, the Turks failed miserably in their first campaign in Russia, losing 70 per cent, dead or wounded, of an army estimated to be at least 100,000 strong. Enver Pasha blamed Turkey's defeat on Armenian deserters who had gone over to the Russian side. Retribution was brutal, resulting in the Armenian massacre, sometimes considered the first genocide, in which Armenians were deported to Syria. Famine, disease and murder resulted in one to two million Armenian deaths.

The British pressed on with their plan for a diversionary attack, which would use the Royal Navy to take control of the Dardanelles

Strait from where they could attack Constantinople, the Ottoman capital. The Dardanelles, a strait of water separating mainland Turkey and the Gallipoli peninsula, is 38 miles long and, at its widest, only 3.5 miles. Britain's First Lord of the Admiralty, Winston Churchill, insisted that the Royal Navy, acting alone, could succeed. On 19 February, a flotilla of British and French ships pounded the outer forts of the Dardanelles and a month later attempted to penetrate the strait. It failed, losing six ships, half its fleet. Soldiers, it was decided, would be needed after all.

Lord Kitchener placed Sir Ian Hamilton in charge, but sent him into battle with out-of-date maps, inaccurate information and inexperienced troops. A force of British, French and ANZAC (Australian and New Zealand Army Corps) troops landed on the Gallipoli peninsula on 25 April. The Turks were waiting for them in the hills above the beaches and unleashed a volley of fire that kept the Allied troops pinned down on the sand. As on the Western Front, stalemate ensued. The Allies, under constant attack, took cover as best they could among the rocks, with only the beach behind them and, without shade, exposed to searing sun. Their fallen comrades lay putrefied and bloated beside them, the stench filling the air.

On 6 August, the British launched a renewed attack. The ANZACs would attempt to break out from their beach and take the high ground whilst a British contingent of 20,000 new troops led by General Sir Frederick Stopford would land on Sulva Bay on the north side of Gallipoli. Stopford's men made a successful landing, outnumbering the enemy by fifteen to one. Instead of pressing home their advantage, the general gave his men the afternoon off to enjoy the sun while he had a snooze. Hamilton advised but did not order an advance. By the time Stopford did advance, it was too late; the Turks had rushed men into position and the stalemate of before prevailed.

The Allied troops endured further months of misery. Seventy per cent of the ANZACs suffered from dysentery, and medical care, unlike on the Western Front, was at best primitive. With the onset of winter, the troops, without shelter and exposed to the elements, suffered frostbite. Kitchener was dispatched by the British government to check on the situation. Appalled, he returned to London and urged evacuation. Finally, in January 1916, the curtain fell on the whole sorry 'side show'. A contrite Churchill resigned and punished himself by joining a company of Royal Scot Fusiliers on the Western Front. He returned to politics a year later and in 1917 was appointed Minister of Munitions. Meanwhile, Kitchener, who had been progressively sidelined, was sent on a diplomatic mission to Russia. On 5 June 1916, his ship, the HMS *Hampshire*, hit a German mine off the Orkney Islands and sank. His body was never found.

During 1915, Germany dangled a bait in front of neutral Bulgaria – help us defeat Serbia and we'll give you Macedonia, territory Bulgaria lost to Serbia after the Balkan War of 1912–13. Unable to resist, the Bulgarian king, the German-born 'Foxy Ferdinand', Ferdinand I, entered the war in October 1915 and immediately joined the German-Austrian assault on Serbia.

Twice, in 1914, Austrian-Hungarian ventures in Serbia had met with defeat. Not this time. In October 1915, the Allies, attempting to aid Serbia, sent a force to the Greek port of Salonika (now Thessaloniki) from where it was only fifty miles to the landlocked Serbia. Too late. Heavily outnumbered, Belgrade fell and the Serbian army was forced into a desperate retreat over the mountains of Albania, struggling in the snow alongside thousands of Serbian refugees. Starvation, cold and disease decimated their number, both soldier and civilian alike. Eventually, the remnants arrived at the Adriatic coast, where they were rescued by the Allies and evacuated to Corfu. Austria-Hungary had avenged the death of Archduke Franz Ferdinand and Serbia had paid for it by losing one-sixth of her whole population.

The Allied troops in Salonika however stayed put to dissuade the Greeks from joining the German cause (after all, they reckoned, the Greek king was married to the Kaiser's sister). And there the Allied troops remained for the rest of the war, half a million men, mocked as 'the Gardeners of Salonika', whose services could have been better used elsewhere. Greece eventually joined the war on the side of the Allies in July 1917.

The Ottoman Empire

In November 1914, the British sent a force to protect the Suez Canal in Egypt from Turkish troops based in Turkish-controlled Palestine. In late January and February 1915, as expected, the Turks tried to seize the canal and again in July 1916, but both assaults were easily repulsed.

Another British force, consisting mainly of Indian troops, occupied Basra in Turkish Mesopotamia (modern-day Iraq) in November 1914 to secure its oil wells. From there, with a hold on Turkish territory, it made sense to extend its gains and capture Baghdad, which would, according to Asquith, 'maintain the authority of our flag in the East'. In August 1915, a force led by General Charles Townsend pushed forward under 43°C heat and, along the way, occupied the town of Kut-el-Amara. Urged to advance to Baghdad, Townsend did so, but, meeting a determined Turkish counter-attack, was forced back to Kut where his men came under siege. With supplies running low and the situation desperate, attempts were made to rescue Townsend but these failed, with a loss of 23,000 lives. After 147 days of siege, starving and unable to hold out, Townsend surrendered on 29 April 1916. His 13,000 men, one third of whom were Indian, were marched off to captivity, where up to 70 per cent were to die of malnutrition.

In December 1916, the British, under General Stanley Maude, made a fresh attempt to capture Baghdad. Maude recaptured Kut and, on 11 March 1917, beat the Turks out of Baghdad. 'Our armies,' proclaimed Maude to the citizens of Baghdad, 'do not come into your cities and lands as conquerors or enemies, but as liberators.'

In January 1917, British troops marched towards Jerusalem, determined to oust Turkey from Palestine. Along the way, the British tried twice to take Gaza and twice failed. The third attempt, in November, led by General Sir Edmund Allenby, was successful, leading to the capture of Jerusalem on 11 December 1917. In January 1916, in a secret agreement known as the Sykes–Picot Agreement (after its authors), the British and French settled on the partition of Palestine and Mesopotamia, at that point still under the rule of the Turkish Ottoman Empire. At the same time, the British were offering bits of Turkey to the Russians, Italians, and the Arabs. The Arabs, accordingly, played their part in the British campaign. Led by the enigmatic T. E. Lawrence, they continuously disrupted Turkish communications through sabotage and guerrilla tactics. On realizing the British had conflicting plans for Palestine, the Arabs felt betrayed, even more so with the Balfour Declaration of November 1917. Britain's foreign secretary, Arthur Balfour, proposed a permanent settlement for Jews within Palestine. The stipulation that 'nothing shall be done which may prejudice the civil and religious rights of existing non-Jewish communities in Palestine' did nothing to allay Arab concerns.

Verdun

In Germany, Falkenhayn decided that Germany's 'arch enemy' was not France, but Britain. But to destroy Britain's will, Germany had first to defeat France. In a 'Christmas memorandum' to the Kaiser, Falkenhayn proposed an offensive that would compel the French to 'throw in every man they have. If they do so,' he continued, 'the forces of France will bleed to death.' The place to do this, Falkenhayn declared, would be Verdun.

An ancient town, Verdun was surrounded by a string of sixty interlocked and reinforced forts. On 21 February 1916, 1,200 German guns pounded the city, which, despite intelligence warning of the impending attack, remained poorly defended. Verdun, symbolically significant to the French, was deemed not so important by the upper echelon of France's military. Joffre was slow to respond until the exasperated French prime minister, Aristide Briand, paid a night-time visit to Joffre, waking him from his slumber and insisting that he take the situation more seriously: 'You may not think losing Verdun a defeat but everyone else will.'

Sent by Joffre, Henri-Philippe Pétain organized a stern defence of the city and managed to protect the only road open to the French. Every day, while under continuous fire, 2,000 lorries made a return trip along the 45-mile Voie Sacrée ('Sacred Way') bringing in vital supplies and reinforcements to be fed into the furnace that Verdun had become. Serving under Pétain was General Robert Nivelle who famously promised that '*on ne passe pas*' (they shall not pass), a quote often attributed to Pétain. Joffre demanded that Haig open up the new offensive on the Somme to take the pressure off his beleaguered men at Verdun. Haig, concerned that the new recruits to the British army were not yet battle-ready, offered 15 August as a start date. Joffre responded angrily that the French army would 'cease to exist' by then. Haig brought forward the offer to 1 July.

During June, the attack and counter-attack at Verdun continued. On the Eastern Front, the Russian general, Aleksei Brusilov, attacked the Austrians, who, in turn, appealed to Falkenhayn for help. Falkenhayn responded by calling a temporary halt at Verdun and transferring men east. The Battle of Verdun wound down, then fizzled out entirely. The French, under the stewardship of Nivelle, regained much of what they had lost. After ten months of fighting, the city had been flattened, and the Germans and French, between them, had lost 260,000 men – one death for every ninety seconds of the battle.

The Russians, in what became known as the Brusilov Offensive, shattered the Austrian army to such an extent that it never fully recovered. With Falkenhayn's Germans coming, Brusilov called for reinforcements of his own – but none came. Brusilov's success against the Austrians was countered by his defeat by the Germans.

Trenches

By 1916, the trench system had become a fixed and elaborate aspect of the war in the west. Front-line trenches were backed by reserve and support lines and consisted of underground bunkers. Life in the trenches became a routine of filth, lice, rats, cold, deprivation, and boredom punctuated with moments of terror. Weeks of living in mud often resulted in trench foot. The Germans, content to secure their defensive positions, built more sophisticated trenches that were deeper, more secure, warmer and, in some instances, boasted electricity. For the Allies, determined to rid the German foe from French or Belgian soil, the trenches were only ever meant to be a temporary improvisation.

The system always favoured defence as was shown time and again throughout the war. Generals, planning their advances, continued to advocate the use of preliminary artillery to pound the enemy's trenches and flatten its barbed wire. Then, having pulverized the enemy's front line, infantry could advance across the expanse of No Man's Land, typically between 100 and 400 metres wide, and engage the enemy, finishing him off by bayonet.

The reality always proved otherwise. The artillery, however sustained, rarely did more than limited damage either to trench or manpower. Men, on the receiving end of artillery, would simply disappear underground into the concrete bunkers only to re-emerge as the infantry approached, and mow them down with machine-gun fire. The gains, if any, were usually minimal, soon reversed and came at a high cost.

The cost on the minds and shattered nerves of the men was also high. Combat stress, or 'shell shock', became a common occurrence. Sympathy for these non-visible wounds was not always forthcoming, especially during the early stages of the war. Eighty thousand British servicemen – 2 per cent of those who saw active service – suffered from forms of shell shock. Men were so traumatized they would forget their own names. For many, unable to cope, running away seemed the only option. The risk was high – the French executed over 600 men for desertion or cowardice, the British and Commonwealth 306, and Germany 18. The US sentenced 24 to death but no executions were carried out.

The Battle of the Somme started with the usual preliminary bombardment. Lasting five days, and involving 1,350 guns, soldiers were assured that the eighteen-mile German front line would be flattened – it would just be a matter of strolling across and taking possession of the German trenches – beyond that lay Berlin.

The British army at the Somme consisted mainly of Kitchener recruits, who had received only minimal training, and were to cross No Man's Land lumbered with almost seventy pounds of equipment. The advance started at 7.30 a.m. on 1 July 1916. To the right of the British was a smaller French force, transferred from Verdun. The men advanced in rigid lines. The German trenches ahead had not been decimated by the artillery but were bristling with guns pointing towards the advance. What followed went down as the worst day in British military history – 57,000 men fell on that first day alone, 19,240 of them lay dead.

One of Britain's generals at the Somme, Sir Beauvoir de Lisle, wrote, 'It was a remarkable display of training and discipline, and the attack failed only because dead men cannot move on.' Despite the appalling losses, Haig decided to 'press [the enemy] hard with the least possible delay'. Thus the attack was resumed the following day – and the day after that.

On 15 September, Haig introduced the modern equivalent of the cavalry onto the battlefield – the tank. Originated in Britain, and championed by Churchill, the term 'tank' was at first merely a codename to conceal its proper name of 'landship'. Despite advice to wait for more testing, Haig had insisted on their use at the Somme. He got his way and the introduction of thirty-two tanks met with mixed results. Many broke down, but a few managed to penetrate German lines. As always, the Germans soon plugged the hole forged by the tanks. Nonetheless, Haig was impressed and immediately ordered a thousand more.

The Battle of the Somme ground on for another two months. Soldiers from every part of the Empire were thrown into the mêlée – Australians, Canadians, New Zealanders, Indians and South Africans all played their part. The battle finally terminated on 18 November, after 140 days of fighting. Approximately 400,000 British lives were lost, 200,000 French, and 400,000 German. For this the Allies gained five miles. The Germans, having been pushed back, merely bolstered the already heavily fortified second line, the Hindenburg Line.

Change at the Top

In Germany, pressure was mounting. A British blockade of German ports was having an effect – resulting in desperate food shortages, food strikes and what the Germans called the 'turnip winter' of 1916–17. The scale of losses at the Somme brought about the sacking of Falkenhayn in August 1916, replaced by the duo that had so much success on the Eastern Front – Hindenburg and Ludendorff.

Falkenhayn was not the only casualty – in December 1916 in France, Joffre was replaced by the popular Robert Nivelle who had made his reputation as Pétain's deputy at Verdun. Nivelle promised he had a scheme which would win the Allies the war within just two days. When Nivelle revealed his plan, it seemed to both the French and British no different from previous strategies. Nivelle threatened to resign. The government, fearing the backlash of the French public, allowed Nivelle free rein.

Changes were afoot in Britain also – Herbert Asquith, too long an impotent leader of a coalition, resigned, to be replaced on 7 December 1916 by former Secretary of State for War, David Lloyd George. Before the war, Lloyd George had been amongst its staunchest opponents and almost resigned on the issue. Asquith persuaded him otherwise but it earned Lloyd George much rancour from within his own party, the Liberals, so that as a coalition prime minister he became overly dependent on the Conservative majority. As the new prime minister, Lloyd George was committed to winning the war – 'The fight must be to the finish – to a knockout blow'– but he would have to work with his commander-in-chief, Haig, whom he disliked and felt had little regard for the lives of his men. When, in February 1917, Lloyd George effectively subjugated Haig and his generals to the French, albeit only for the duration of Nivelle's offensive, he also earned the animosity of Haig.

Part of Nivelle's grand plan was to distract the Germans with an offensive designed to relieve the stricken city of Arras, in France. The Germans had deeply entrenched themselves in the high ground of Vimy Ridge surrounding the city back in September 1914, and had pounded the city ever since. Previous attempts to dislodge the Germans had failed. On 12 April 1917, after four days of fighting, a force of British, ANZACs and Canadians managed to regain the ridge. Despite the success at Vimy Ridge, elsewhere the Germans counter-attacked and the familiar pattern reasserted itself.

A week later, on 16 April, Nivelle launched his main offensive on which he had staked his reputation. The Second Battle of the Aisne was doomed to failure from the start. Nivelle's carefully laid plans had fallen into the hands of the Germans who prepared accordingly. The introduction of French tanks had no effect, and French artillery fell on their own infantry. The losses were huge. Nivelle's promise of a 48-hour victory evaporated as the battle continued on for two weeks and petered out in early May. Nivelle, briefly the would-be saviour of France, was sacked and replaced by his former boss, Philippe Pétain, a man who was unusually sympathetic to the plight of his men. It was just as well because within the army were the first murmurs of dissent.

From dissent came mutiny. In May 1917, French soldiers refused to fight any more. The word spread and thousands deserted. Fortunately for Pétain, his front-line troops remained in place. Behind the lines, men, worn down by war, filthy conditions, and the lack of sufficient medical care, refused to obey orders or return to the front. Painstakingly, Pétain managed to restore order through a combination of the carrot and stick. Ringleaders were arrested, court-martialled and, in forty-three cases, executed. In the longer term, Pétain doubled a soldier's length of leave, improved conditions, food and welfare. Most importantly, Pétain promised the French soldier that there would be no more pointless offensives or risks taken, until both the Americans had arrived and tanks were in full supply.

Air and Sea

Aircraft developed substantially during the war. They were initially used for observation and reconnaissance, until the French became the first to attach a machine gun to a plane. It was a Dutchman, working for the Germans, Anton Fokker, who provided the solution for firing a machine gun through a propeller. With the development of the fighter plane came the concept of dogfights, and 'aces' on all sides achieved celebrity status for their acts of daring, the most renowned being the German, Manfred von Richthofen, the Red Baron. Richthofen, credited with a record eighty kills, was shot down and killed in April 1918.

Bomber planes caused damage to major cities such as London, Paris and Cologne. Paris, for example, suffered 266 deaths throughout the war from aerial bombardment, be it aeroplane or zeppelin. In Britain the Royal Flying Corps was an adjunct to the army until, on 1 April 1918, in recognition of the growing importance of aerial combat, it merged with the Royal Navy Air Service to form the Royal Air Force.

On 31 May 1916, the largest sea battle took place – the Battle of Jutland. Chief Admiral of the German High Seas Fleet, Reinhard Scheer, knew full well that Britain boasted the strongest navy, but believed he could lure individual ships into battle and deal with the British fleet one vessel at a time. His grandiose plans however went awry when Britain deciphered the enemy's communications, discovering exactly what Scheer had in mind. The battle around the Danish waters of Jutland, led by Scheer and his British counterpart, Admiral Sir John Jellicoe, proved a cat and mouse affair with no clear victor, although by sheer numbers of ships sunk, the Germans claimed the honours. The clashes of big ships however came to an end. German strategy changed to greater reliance on the submarine. In January 1917, the Germans issued a proclamation that her U-boats would, thenceforth, attack anything in sight on the east side of the Atlantic, without warning, whether neutral or not. Their idea was to prevent food and supplies reaching Britain. Within a month, German U-boats had sunk five US ships, killing American passengers.

The U-boats were decimating shipping crossing the Atlantic, sinking 25 per cent of British merchant ships bringing in essential supplies and foodstuffs. Admiral Jellicoe warned 'it is impossible for us to go on with the war if losses like this continue'. Lloyd George's answer was to implement a system of convoys so that ships would not have to run the gauntlet of travelling alone. Introduced in May 1917, the effect was immediate – the losses to British ships went down from a quarter to one per cent.

Ireland and Easter Monday

In 1914, Ireland had been on the brink of civil war – the Government Act of Ireland (or, Third Home Rule Bill) had just been passed by Asquith's Liberal government, but its implementation was to be delayed until the cessation of war. Both Unionists and Nationalists volunteered to fight for Britain, each side hoping that by answering Britain's call-to-arms, they would be rewarded by Whitehall after the war.

The Unionists were keen to demonstrate their loyalty, while the Nationalists hoped to prove they were not so anti-British that they could not be trusted with Home Rule. A minority of about 10,000 Nationalists, however, resented their colleagues' kowtowing to the British and planned on an uprising to take place on Easter Monday, 24 April 1916. The uprising had limited success and many viewed it as a traitorous act while their brothers were fighting for the British. Britain squandered its sympathetic support in Ireland by its harsh suppression and punishment of the uprising's leaders and participants.

Russia and Revolution

Following a series of defeats on the Eastern Front, Tsar Nicholas II dismissed his commander-in-chief, perhaps under the influence of the Russian mystic and soothsayer, Grigori Rasputin. Nicholas appointed himself in charge of Russia's future war effort, despite his total lack of military experience.

On 8 March 1917 the culmination of food shortages, dissatisfaction with the war and public discontent all contributed to an uprising in the Russian city of Petrograd. The city, formerly St Petersburg, had been renamed to the less Germanic-sounding Petrograd in 1914. By 12 March, there was revolution. Two million Russian soldiers deserted in the eight weeks of March and April alone. Soldiers, previously loyal to the Tsar, joined the movement. Nicholas tried to return to the city but found his way barred. The Russians had become disillusioned with their Tsar and his domineering wife who, they felt, paid too much heed to Rasputin.

Having, in a matter of days, lost all authority, the Tsar abdicated. The three-century-old Romanov dynasty was no more. The Tsar, his wife, family and household were all executed by the Bolsheviks in Yekaterinburg on 17 July 1918.

In place of the monarchy, a provisional government, under Alexander Kerensky, had no intention of suing for peace, and instead promised that the new government would do 'everything in its power to carry the war to a victorious conclusion'. However, Kerensky's authority was undermined by workers' councils, or 'Soviets', that had sprung up in the cities. One man, in exile in Zurich, was determined to end the war and bring about an international workers' revolution. The Germans, keen to allow him to cause as much discord in Russia as possible, gave him passage back to his native land through Germany in a sealed train. His name was Vladimir Lenin.

Arriving in Petrograd on 16 April, he was soon joined by fellow revolutionary, Leon Trotsky. Lenin immediately went on the offensive – denouncing Kerensky, the war and the exploitation of Russia's peasants, workers and soldiers.

In July, Kerensky launched the Russian army against the Germans, the Kerensky Offensive, but it failed. The Germans counter-attacked and advanced as far as Riga. This was the final straw for the Russian soldier.

In Petrograd, Kerensky went on the attack – arresting Bolsheviks, including Trotsky, and trying to restore order. Lenin disappeared to Finland and went into hiding. Kerensky's commander-in-chief, Lavr Kornilov, was heading back to the city, fresh from his defeat by the Germans, with the intention of taking control. Kerensky released the Bolsheviks and begged Lenin to return. Kornilov's soldiers were met by the revolutionaries at the gates of Petrograd and persuaded to down their weapons. They did – many went home; others joined the Bolsheviks. Kornilov was arrested.

On 7 November (or 25 October by the old Russian calendar), the Bolsheviks seized control of the Winter Palace, arrested members of the provisional government and declared Lenin their chairman.

Lenin and Trotsky now set about their mission to change Russia, freeing the workers and peasants from the chains of capitalism. Lenin proclaimed his Decree on Peace, inviting all belligerent nations to lay down their arms. Only Germany took him up on his offer. The armistice that officially ended the war between Russia and Germany, and her allies, was signed on 16 December, leading to negotiations at Brest-Litovsk in eastern Poland.

Germany's demands of Russia were severe – the secession of Poland, Finland, Estonia, Latvia, Lithuania, and the Ukraine to the German empire – almost 30 per cent of its population. Even the Bolsheviks baulked at this and walked out of the talks. The German army prepared to make its point with a renewal of war. Lenin ordered Trotsky to sign. So on 3 March 1918, Trotsky returned to the table and signed the hated agreement, the Treaty of Brest-Litovsk.

Germany had at last a war on one front but Ludendorff had to station a million men on the Eastern Front to discourage the Russians from revoking the treaty. Nonetheless, he was still able to transfer the bulk to the Western Front, giving the Germans a numerical superiority over the Allies. It would not last long.

Russia now had a communist government. It may have lost vast swathes of territory and a sizeable bulk of its population but it had freed itself from the war. Instead, it descended into a civil war between the Bolsheviks and the counter-revolutionaries that was to last five long years.

USA

Germany compounded the error of sinking US ships with its U-boats by trying to draw Mexico into an alliance. In January 1917, the German Foreign Secretary, Arthur Zimmermann, sent a telegram to the German ambassador in Mexico with instructions to open negotiations with the Mexicans. He was to offer help to restore territories lost by Mexico to the US in the nineteenth century, namely New Mexico, Texas, and Arizona. The Zimmermann Telegram however was intercepted by the British. Decoded and published in their newspapers, it enraged US public opinion against Germany. On 6 April 1917, the US declared war on Germany, and their president, Woodrow Wilson, in his declaration, talked of making the 'world safe for democracy'. The Allies, although delighted by this latest development, knew it would be many months before the US, with its small and poorly equipped army, would be fully prepared and battle-ready.

On 8 January 1918, in a speech to Congress, Wilson delivered his Fourteen Points, a programme for peace based on the principles of democracy and justice and not on punishment and reparations. Wilson hoped it would encourage the Central Powers to seek peace. Georges Clemenceau, the new French prime minister, was scathing – 'Fourteen? The good Lord had only ten.'

Passchendaele

While Pétain was waiting for tanks and Americans, and determined not to expose his men to any more fruitless offensives, the onus fell on Britain. Unfortunately for the British soldier, Haig was convinced that a breakthrough was still possible and argued for another great offensive. Pétain advised against it. As did Haig's own staff. Lloyd George, too, was utterly opposed. But Haig had got the backing of the Conservatives within Lloyd George's coalition and so got his way.

It started well in June 1917 at Messines Ridge, near Ypres. The British had spent two years tunnelling underground down to a depth of 100 feet (32 metres). The Germans were digging in the opposite direction, slightly higher up. Sometimes, they came so close they could hear each other. Made using only hand-held tools, it was an amazing feat of engineering. They dug twenty-two mines in a position beneath the German-held ridge, and stuffed them with explosives. At 3.10, on the morning of 7 June, the mines were detonated all at once. Three failed to explode but the combined blast of the other nineteen was so loud as to be heard by Lloyd George asleep in Downing Street and as far away as Dublin. Ten thousand Germans were killed in a trice.

On 31 July, Haig launched his main attack, the Third Battle of Ypres, otherwise known as the Battle of Passchendaele. Soon the rains came, and within no time the battle scene had degenerated into a sea of mud – guns disappeared into it, tanks sank in it, a quarter of the men killed at Passchendaele drowned in it. In August, Lloyd George personally came to visit the front line. The prime minister despaired but failed to stop its continuation. The battle wore on for another three months. On 20 November, the Canadians captured the town of Passchendaele itself and the battle finally halted. Some 250,000 Allies had been killed or wounded; 200,000 Germans.

On 20 November, tanks, which had proved so impractical in the mud of Passchendaele, attacked the Germans at Cambrai. There was no preliminary bombardment to warn the Germans and, for once, the British achieved a victory that could be measured in miles as opposed to feet. The public at home was delighted – for the first time, church bells rang out in celebration. Within a week, the Germans recaptured the lost ground. Nothing had changed. The bells never rang again.

The Spring Offensive, 1918

Lenin had hoped that workers everywhere among the belligerent nations would follow Russia's lead. January 1918 saw massive workers' strikes in Berlin and other German cities and although the strikes shook the establishment, revolution did not follow. But it was enough to stir Germany into further military action. The Russians may have been out of the war but the Americans were due soon and neither the German public nor the German economy would stand for much more. Ludendorff planned the last throw of the dice.

At 4.40 a.m. on 21 March 1918, the Germans launched their 'Spring Offensive' on Allied positions on the Somme. In the first five hours the Germans fired over a million shells. The initial breakthrough of nearly fifty miles was spectacular. Ludendorff ordered his men westwards towards the important rail junction of Amiens. The Germans were jubilant, the Kaiser arranged for a 'Victory' holiday. Further south, the Germans deployed their new big artillery guns, the 'Big

Berthas', and bombed Paris from a distance of seventy-five miles.

On 26 March, French general, Ferdinand Foch, was elevated to become the 'Allied Supreme Commander of the Western Front', leapfrogging Pétain and Haig. Foch accepted the position with a declaration of his intentions: 'I would fight without a break . . . I would fight all the time. I would never surrender.'

Around Amiens, the Allies held the Germans in check, just ten miles short of the city. Instead, the Germans thrust on towards Hazebrouck, near the Belgian border. On 12 April, fearing for the safety of the Channel ports, Haig issued his famous order, 'With our backs to the wall and believing in the justice of our cause, each one of us must fight to the end.' The Germans beat a consignment of Portuguese and re-took Passchendaele.

The war had suddenly become a war of movement again and both sides had problems overcoming the logistical difficulties of maintaining supplies. Now, the Americans had finally landed – initially with 180,000 troops, led by their commander, General John 'Black Jack' Pershing.

Ludendorff decided the momentum had to be maintained. On 27 May, he struck at the southern end of the Western Front, over the River Aisne. By 30 May, the Germans had reached the River Marne and were now just forty miles from Paris. But again the Germans were checked, most notably in the Battle of Belleau Wood, where they were beaten back by a unit of US marines. At one point, the French, advising the US commander to retreat, received the reply, 'Retreat? Hell, we just got here.'

In the midst of war, troops on all sides were being decimated by a global pandemic of what became known as Spanish flu. Perhaps the biggest pandemic in history, it affected a fifth of the world's population and killed 50 to 100 million people. Soldiers were particularly susceptible, given their levels of fatigue and stress, their lack of cleanliness and unhealthy living conditions.

The Hundred Days

Exhausted and demoralized, the last German offensive had come to an end. Now, instead, they faced the Allies' 'Hundred Days' counter-offensive. Starting on 18 July, the Allies pushed the Germans back beyond the River Marne. German dreams of reaching Paris were dead. The Battle of Amiens on 8 August saw the Germans lose 30,000 men, in what Ludendorff described in his post-war diaries as a 'black day for the German army'. By the beginning of September the Germans were back on their Hindenburg Line, from where they had started their Spring Offensive almost six months previously. German soldiers were deserting or being taken prisoner of war at alarming rates. Huge numbers succumbed to the Spanish flu.

On 29 September, Bulgaria became the first of Germany's allies to surrender, its king, Ferdinand I, abdicating. Domestically, revolution in Germany was looming. Ludendorff wanted to accept

Wilson's Fourteen Points and its promise of non-punitive measures, a plan which the British and the French found far too lenient. Ludendorff urged also, in order to strengthen the German cause, the introduction of a 'government [with] a broader foundation'. It was a devious move on Ludendorff's part – pass the responsibility for a German surrender to a parliamentary government and then let them, not the military, take the blame for the nation's defeat.

On 3 October the Kaiser duly appointed the liberal Prince Maximilian of Baden Chancellor of Germany. But it was not enough for Wilson – he demanded the Kaiser's abdication. This was too much for Ludendorff who, having previously said the war was lost, was now keen to maintain hostilities. On 26 October he was dismissed.

Elsewhere Germany's allies were falling. The year before, in October 1917, a joint German and Austrian-Hungarian offensive won the Battle of Caporetto against the Italians. It was a devastating blow for the Italians, who were pushed back to the River Piave, only fifteen miles from Venice.

In June 1918, the Austrian-Hungarians had tried but failed to destroy the Italians. The Italians waited four months before counter-attacking, by which time Germany was no longer in a position to offer its ally reinforcements. During the course of the Battle of Vittorio Veneto, the Austrian-Hungarian empire as a political entity collapsed. On 28 October, Czechoslovakia declared its independence from the empire. The following day, the South Slavs did likewise, and was soon to become Yugoslavia. Hungary followed suit on 31 October. Austria signed an armistice on 3 November, and the Habsburg monarchy was no more. For Italy also, the war was over.

Turkey also surrendered. Damascus, part of the Ottoman Empire for 400 years, fell to the British on 1 October. More defeats followed and finally, on 30 October, Turkey signed an armistice. The once powerful and far-reaching Ottoman Empire was finished.

German admirals, defiant and not ready to accept defeat, prepared to send their fleets out once more to do battle against the Royal Navy. On 29 October, sailors based in Kiel, sensing this to be a futile and suicidal mission, mutinied. The mutiny quickly spread, the province of Bavaria establishing a Socialist republic along Soviet lines. For the new German government, a stop to hostilities was now a necessity not just to end the war but also to avert revolution.

Armistice

Hindenburg and Wilhelm Groener (Ludendorff's replacement) went to see the Kaiser who had bolted to army headquarters in the Belgian town of Spa. Hindenburg, the monarchist, bowed his head in shame and left Groener to do the talking. The Kaiser remained defiant until the news came through: in Berlin, Prince Max had proclaimed a Socialist republic and had passed the chancellorship to the Social Democrat, Friedrich Ebert. Thus, on 10 November, Kaiser Wilhelm II abdicated. The 500-year rule of the Hohenzollern dynasty had come to an end. The Kaiser fled to the Netherlands and into exile, never again to step on German soil.

On 9 November, Matthias Erzberger, representing Ebert's new government, met Foch and the French delegation in a railway carriage in the woods of Compiègne. Erzberger had come to seek an armistice; Foch to dictate its terms. Wilson's Fourteen Points of leniency had gone – instead the French made such demands that Erzberger protested. Germany would have to forgo most of its military, large swathes of territory, and annul the Treaty of Brest-Litovsk. From Berlin, Ebert brushed aside Erzberger's protests and told him to sign.

Signed at 5 a.m., Paris time, the Western Front Armistice came into effect at 11 a.m. – 'the eleventh hour of the eleventh day of the eleventh month'. Tragically, during the intervening six hours there were many more deaths. The last recorded death was that of a US soldier, 23-year-old Henry Gunther; as he charged, bayonet drawn, astonished German troops tried to warn him, before shooting him down. The time was 10.59. 'Almost as he fell, the gunfire died away and an appalling silence prevailed.'

Paris Peace Conference

The Paris Peace Conference opened on 18 January 1919. Thirty-two countries were represented, including the new nations that had emerged from the break-up of the Austrian-Hungarian empire, but proceedings were dominated by Woodrow Wilson, Georges Clemenceau and David Lloyd George.

The conference produced five treaties, one for each of the defeated Central Powers, none of whom were in attendance, and each named after a Parisian suburb. The Treaty of Sèvres officially closed down the Ottoman Empire and virtually abolished Turkish sovereignty. The Turkish government was ready to sign but followers of the nationalist leader Mustafa Kemal rebelled. The resultant Turkish War of Independence saw Kemal come to power to establish the Republic of Turkey in 1923. The Treaty of Trianon imposed strict punishments on Hungary. New boundaries were drawn in the Balkans, the Middle East and Africa.

Italy, lured into war by territorial promises, was treated dismissively during talks, causing its prime minister, Vittorio Orlando, to walk out. Italy was disappointed by its spoils of war. Orlando, heavily criticized by Italy's rising right, led by Benito Mussolini, was soon ousted.

The terms of the German treaty, the Treaty of Versailles, were particularly harsh. On being presented with the document, Germany was given three weeks to comply. The German government complained that Wilson's Fourteen Points had largely been ignored – with the exception of Wilson's proposal to form a League of Nations. They argued that, having not been consulted, the terms were nothing less than a dictate. Ultimately, however, the German government was too weak to do anything but add its signature, which they did, on 28 June 1919, exactly five years after the assassination of Archduke Franz Ferdinand.

As a result of the treaty, Germany lost 13 per cent of its territory and all its colonies, the Rhineland was to be demilitarized, its army limited to a token 100,000 men and its navy to 15,000. The treaty declared Germany and its allies responsible for all 'loss and damage' caused during the war, for which it would have to pay reparations. The amount, announced two years later, was set at 132 billion marks (the equivalent today of about $440 billion or £210 billion). But it was Article 231, the 'War Guilt Clause', that caused the German public the greatest humiliation – forced into admitting that the whole conflict had been the fault of Germany. Foch said, 'This isn't a peace. It's a ceasefire for twenty years.'

The War to End War?

The Treaty of Versailles, as well as causing deep resentment in Germany, satisfied none of the Allies. The British, who wanted to see Germany punished but not destroyed, felt the treaty too harsh. The French – having borne the brunt of the conflict – were determined to see Germany destroyed and thought it too weak. Within six months, Clemenceau, who became a scapegoat for France's disappointment, was voted out of office. Wilson returned to the US to find a country increasingly isolationist in its outlook. The Senate neither ratified the Treaty nor joined the League of Nations.

Germans throughout the country rounded on the politicians who had signed the Treaty. The war had been lost, not by the German army, they claimed, but by the politicians – the government had 'stabbed the nation in the back'. After all, not since 1914 had a single foreign soldier stepped on German soil. H. G. Wells had coined the phrase 'the war to end war', used also by Wilson, but Lloyd George was more accurate when, mockingly, he said, 'This war, like the next war, is a war to end war.'

The Weimar Republic came into being in February 1919, but the humiliation of defeat, the perceived treachery of Germany, and social and political discontent remained rampant. One ex-corporal spoke for many when he summed up the shame of Germany's defeat. On the day of the Armistice, the soldier had been in a hospital recovering from a gas attack. He described how he sobbed into his pillow, blaming the 'gang of wretched criminals' that had betrayed the fatherland. 'Hatred grew in me,' he wrote, 'hatred for those responsible for this deed.' His name was Adolf Hitler.

Appendix One: Key Players

The Three Kings

King George V of Britain, Kaiser Wilhelm II of Germany, and Tsar Nicholas II of Russia (Georgie, Willy and Nicky) were all cousins. George and Wilhelm were both grandsons of Queen Victoria and Nicholas's wife, the Empress Alexandra, was her granddaughter. They met, as a threesome, only twice. All three were considered feckless.

Kaiser Wilhelm II

Arrogant, extremely vain, and always seeking praise, Wilhelm II enjoyed a life of frivolity. His former chancellor, Otto von Bismarck, once remarked that the Kaiser would have liked every day to be his birthday. Much to Wilhelm's delight, Queen Victoria made her grandson an honorary admiral of the Royal Navy for which, he said, he would always take an interest in Britain's fleet as if it was his own. Born with a paralysed left arm, considerably shorter than the right, Wilhelm needed help with eating and dressing throughout his life, and went to great lengths to hide his disability.

A lover of all things military and a collector of uniforms (he owned 600, many of which he designed himself), Wilhelm's knowledge of military matters was little more than that of an overenthusiastic schoolchild. During the war, his ministers and generals bypassed him, and Ludendorff, especially, became a *de facto* ruler of the country.

Following the war and his forced abdication, Wilhelm lived in exile in the Netherlands. His cousin, King George, described him as 'the greatest criminal in history'. The Dutch queen, Queen Wilhelmina, declined ever to meet the fallen Kaiser but when the Paris Peace Conference requested Wilhelm's extradition to face trial for war crimes, she refused.

In 1940, with Hitler's armies bearing down on the Netherlands, the Dutch Royal Family fled to Britain. Wilhelm however did not, even refusing Winston Churchill's offer of asylum. He preferred instead to live under German occupation, hoping that the Nazis would restore the monarchy. He died the following year.

Tsar Nicholas II

Nicholas II believed he ruled Russia by divine right and could see no other way but rule by autocracy. He paid little heed to either his advisers or his people, and ignored the political and social unrest fermenting in Russia. That he was despised and considered an anachronism had no effect on the Tsar. No believer in change, he undid the minor reforms he felt obliged to implement following the failed Russian Revolution of 1905.

Following Russian reversals during the early stages of the First World War, he took personal command of Russia's military, despite having no experience of military matters. It was a fatal error of judgement – because he could no longer blame his generals for the failure of Russia's armies, defeat was now his personal responsibility. He left the running of the country to his wife, Alexandra, who, in turn, was overly influenced by the mercurial mystic, Grigori Rasputin. This, together with the growing disillusionment of war, did nothing to help the Tsar's cause.

Forced to abdicate in March 1917, following the February

Revolution, Nicholas and his family and immediate entourage were imprisoned and held in various safe houses. The British government wanted to offer Nicholas asylum but King George, his cousin, refused it, fearing that the presence of the fallen Tsar in Britain could cause trouble.

On the night of 18 July 1918, they were all shot by the Bolsheviks, probably on the order of Lenin.

King George V

When, in 1917, King George V changed the family name from Saxe-Coburg-Gotha to Windsor, his cousin, Wilhelm II, joked, 'I look forward to seeing the Merry Wives of Saxe-Coburg-Gotha.' George preferred shooting and stamp collecting to being in the company of politicians or intellectuals. Nor were politicians and intellectuals terribly impressed by the King. During his coronation in 1911, the English writer and caricaturist, Max Beerbohm, dismissed the King as 'such a piteous, good, feeble, heroic little figure'. And David Lloyd George, on first meeting him, said, 'The King is a very jolly chap … thank God there is not much in his head.'

Of the three cousins, George wielded the least power but consequently was the only one to survive in post. He died in 1936 to be succeeded by Edward VIII.

Horatio Kitchener 1850–1916

Lord Kitchener's face and pointing finger proclaiming 'Your country needs you', often copied and mimicked, is one of the most recognizable posters of all time.

Born in County Kerry, Ireland, Kitchener first saw active service with the French army during the Franco-Prussian War of 1870–71 and, a decade later, with the British army during the occupation of Egypt. He was part of the force that tried, unsuccessfully, to relieve General Charles Gordon, besieged in Khartoum in 1885. The death of Gordon, at the hands of Mahdist forces, caused great anguish in Britain. As commander-in-chief of the Egyptian army, Kitchener led the campaign of reprisal into the Sudan, defeating the Mahdists at the Battle of Omdurman and reoccupying Khartoum in 1898. Kitchener had restored Britain's pride.

His reputation took a dent however during the Second Boer War in South Africa, 1899–1902. Succeeding Lord Roberts as commander-in-chief, Kitchener resorted to a scorched-earth policy in order to defeat the guerrilla tactics of the Boers. Controversially, he also set up a system of concentration camps and interned Boer women and children and black Africans. Overcrowded, lacking hygiene and malnourished, over 25,000 were to die, for which Kitchener was heavily criticized.

The criticism, however, did not damage Kitchener's career. He became commander-in-chief of India, was promoted to field marshal, and, in 1911, Consul-General of Egypt, responsible, in effect, for governing the whole country.

At the outbreak of hostilities in 1914, Kitchener was appointed Secretary of State for War, the first soldier to hold the post, serving under Asquith's Liberal government. Bleakly, he predicted a long war, a lone voice among the government and military elite, for which Britain would need an army far larger than the existing 1914 professional army, the British Expeditionary Force (BEF). So Kitchener spearheaded a recruitment drive, appearing himself on the iconic poster. Hugely successful, Kitchener's campaign recruited three million volunteers.

Popular with the public but less so with the government, Kitchener lost prestige with the failure of the Gallipoli campaign.

In June 1916, Kitchener was sent on a diplomatic mission to Russia aboard the HMS *Hampshire*. On 5 June, the ship hit a German mine off the Orkney Islands and sank. Kitchener's body was never found, leading to several conspiracy theories that he had become too much of an embarrassment and liability, and had been assassinated. David Lloyd George, then Minister for Munitions, was supposed to have been accompanying Kitchener but cancelled at the last minute – this merely added to the speculation.

Winston Churchill 1874–1965

Churchill admitted in 1915 to enjoying the war – in a letter to Lloyd George's daughter, he wrote, 'I know it's smashing and shattering the lives of thousands every moment, and yet, I can't help it, I enjoy every second of it.'

Academically weak, Churchill sought a career in the army, but took three attempts to pass the entrance exam for the Royal Military College in Sandhurst. In 1896, he served briefly on India's North-West Frontier, writing up his experiences in a series of dispatches that brought him much attention. Churchill served as a cavalry officer during Lord Kitchener's retaliatory campaign in the Sudan and took part in one of the last cavalry charges during the Battle of Omdurman in 1898.

In 1899, Churchill went to South Africa during the Second Boer War, working as a correspondent for *The Morning Post*, but was captured by the Boers and interned in a prisoner-of-war camp. Following a daring escape, he later joined the British army on its way to relieve the British garrison besieged in the city of Ladysmith.

Churchill became a politician in 1900, serving as a Conservative Member of Parliament before swapping sides and joining the Liberal Party in 1904. He served for a year as Home Secretary during which time he became an advocate for eugenics, proposing compulsory sterilization for the 'feeble-minded' and separate labour camps for 'tramps and wastrels'.

In 1911, Churchill was appointed First Lord of the Admiralty. Continuing the policy established by his predecessor, Churchill, determined to keep Britain ahead of the Germans, expanded the navy by introducing dreadnoughts, the most powerful battleships of the time.

Throughout the war, Churchill furthered the cause of the newly developed 'landships', or tanks. It was in his capacity within the Admiralty that Churchill pushed for a navy-only assault on the Dardanelles. Its failure to deliver, and the consequent disaster of Gallipoli, was a severe setback to Churchill's reputation. Demoted and demoralized, Churchill handed in his resignation from the coalition government and, although he remained an MP, joined the front-line troops as a lieutenant colonel on the Western Front. By all accounts, he was popular and courageous and ventured thirty times or so into No Man's Land.

After four months in France, Churchill returned to London and within a couple of months, despite Conservative protests, was appointed Minister for Munitions.

Following the war, in January 1919, Churchill became Secretary of State for War, and, deeply alarmed by the Bolshevik threat, supplied more troops to fight for the counter-revolutionary cause during the Russian Civil War.

Losing his seat as a Liberal MP, Churchill again swapped sides and served a Conservative government as Chancellor of the Exchequer until their defeat in the election of 1929. Although the Conservatives were re-elected in 1931, Churchill, considered too much of a loose cannon, was sidelined. He remained in the shadows throughout the thirties, writing and painting, until recalled to the Admiralty in 1939, by which time the Second World War had begun.

Douglas Haig 1861–1928

Born in Edinburgh, Haig, an expert horseman, once represented England at polo. In 1898, he joined Kitchener's force in the Sudan. Asked by Kitchener's superiors in London to report back in confidence on his commander, Haig did so with relish, taking delight in criticizing the unsuspecting Kitchener. In 1899, Haig served under Sir John French in Kitchener's army during the Boer War in South Africa.

By August 1914, Haig served as a deputy to French who had become commander-in-chief of the BEF. Haig's actions at Mons and the First Battle of Ypres earned him praise while, conversely, French's fortunes plummeted as the British failed to make any headway on the Western Front. Haig helped manoeuvre the mood-swinging French out of power and was appointed by Prime Minister Asquith as French's replacement in December 1915.

Firmly believing that God was on his side and therefore his decisions had to be right, Haig insisted on full-frontal attacks, convinced that victory would come by military might alone. Still a cavalryman at heart, he believed the machine gun to be a 'much overrated weapon'. Haig's tenure as commander-in-chief saw the horrendous losses at the Battle of the Somme and the Third Battle of Ypres (Passchendaele). But Haig had to act under pressure of his French allies, bringing forward, for example, the Somme offensive by six weeks. Despite having a personal rapport with the King, Haig never enjoyed the confidence of Lloyd George, who was openly critical of Haig's cavalier attitude with his men's lives. In 1918, Haig oversaw Britain's advance during the Hundred Days Offensive, pushing back the Germans' Spring Offensive, which, ultimately, led to victory.

After the war, Haig helped establish the British Legion, becoming its first president, a post he held until his death, and also introduced the poppy of remembrance into Britain. He died from a heart attack brought on, according to his widow, by the strain of wartime command. He was sixty-six.

Henri Philippe Pétain 1856–1951

Pétain began the First World War as a general but his successes during 1914 and later at Verdun brought him to public attention. In December 1916, following the sacking of Joseph Joffre, Pétain was passed over for the post of commander-in-chief in favour of his second-in-command at Verdun, Robert Nivelle. Pétain eventually got his chance following the failure of the Nivelle Offensive in April 1917, and in May was made commander-in-chief of French forces. His first task was to quell the French mutiny, which he did through a mixture of discipline and reform. Pétain limited French offensives to the minimum, claiming he was waiting for 'the tanks and the Americans'. He remained the French commander-in-chief but from March 1918 became subordinate to Ferdinand Foch who was appointed the generalissimo of all Allied forces on the Western Front.

In June 1940, during the Second World War, the 84-year-old Pétain was appointed prime minister. His first task was the surrender of the French to the forces of Nazi Germany. The Germans occupied two-fifths of France and Pétain, administering the rest of the country on behalf of the Germans, moved his government to the town of Vichy. In November 1942, the Germans took over the whole country, leaving Pétain little more than a puppet. Following France's liberation in September 1944, Pétain was forced by the Germans to retreat to the German town of Sigmaringen to form a government-in-exile.

In April 1945, Pétain was arrested and put on trial for treason. The court found him guilty and sentenced him to death. But

Charles de Gaulle, taking into account Pétain's age and his First World War record, commuted the sentence to life imprisonment. Pétain was imprisoned, in relative luxury, on the île d'Yeu, on the west coast of France. Increasingly frail, he needed constant care. He died in 1951, aged ninety-five.

Georges Clemenceau 1841–1929

Nicknamed the Tiger for his fiery temperament, Clemenceau was not averse to settling personal feuds by duel. A staunch republican and troublemaker, Clemenceau was once imprisoned for seventy-seven days by Napoleon III's government. In 1865, fearing another arrest, Clemenceau fled to the US where he worked as a journalist and teacher. Following France's defeat during the Franco-Prussian War of 1870–71, Clemenceau opposed France's colonial ambitions, arguing that the country needed to concentrate its efforts on exacting revenge on the Germans.

Clemenceau served as prime minister between 1906 and 1909, and became known for his firmness and his hard stance against the Socialists. During the early part of the First World War, Clemenceau became a vocal critic of France's strategy. Appointed in November 1917 for a second term as prime minister, leading a coalition government, he oversaw France's role in the eventual defeat of Germany.

He took a firm line in the subsequent Paris Peace Conference, determined to see Germany crippled to prevent it from ever again becoming a military threat. Although the conference had largely rejected Woodrow Wilson's conciliatory Fourteen Points, Clemenceau still had to compromise. The French public, dissatisfied with their prime minister's performance, voted him out of office in 1920.

In his latter years, Clemenceau warned against a resurgent Germany, predicting a new war by 1940. He died in 1929.

Gavrilo Princip 1894–1918

Born to an impoverished family in Bosnia in 1894, Princip was one of nine children, six of whom died during infancy. Suffering from tuberculosis, the frail and slight Princip learnt to read, the first in his family to do so, and devoured the histories of the Serbs and their oppression at the hands of the Ottoman and Habsburg Empires.

In 1911, a friend of Princip's, Bogdan Zerajic, had tried to assassinate the Austrian-Hungarian governor of Bosnia. He failed and shot himself. But it provided the young Princip with inspiration. He tried to enlist in various terrorist groups but was turned down due to his short stature. Eventually he was accepted and tasked to join a group called the Black Hand. Its explicit purpose was the assassination of the heir to the Austrian-Hungarian throne, the Archduke Franz Ferdinand. Each member of the gang was given a vial of cyanide in order to kill themselves afterwards.

The plan to assassinate Franz Ferdinand was known to the Serbian prime minister. Although sympathetic, he feared the consequences and ordered the arrest of the Black Hand conspirators. His orders came too late. Having assassinated the Archduke and his wife, Princip tried to shoot himself but was wrestled to the ground where again he tried to kill himself by swallowing his cyanide pill but the poison, so old, failed to work.

At the time of the assassination, Princip was a month short of his twentieth birthday. His age saved him from execution as Austrian-Hungarian law decreed that the death penalty could not be applied to those aged under twenty. Princip therefore was sentenced to the maximum penalty of twenty years. While in prison, he suffered a resurgence of his tuberculosis and, due to the poor hygiene and his inadequate diet, had to have an arm amputated. His condition worsened and he died, aged twenty-three, on 28 April 1918.

Paul von Hindenburg 1847–1934

Hindenburg had had a successful if not spectacular career in the army, decorated in the Austro-Prussian War (1866) and the Franco-Prussian War (1870–71) and retired in 1911.

With the outbreak of war in 1914, Hindenburg was recalled to service, and, with Ludendorff as his deputy, scored an impressive double victory against the Russians at the Battles of Tannenberg and the Masurian Lakes. But a total victory against the Russians was not forthcoming, which Hindenburg blamed entirely on Falkenhayn and his excessive need for troops on the Western Front.

In August 1916, Hindenburg and Ludendorff replaced Falkenhayn. With the Kaiser increasingly sidelined, the duo ran a virtual military regime. Hindenburg implemented Germany's policy of unrestricted submarine warfare, dictated the harsh terms of the Treaty of Brest-Litovsk and helped Ludendorff launch the Spring Offensive of 1918.

A monarchist at heart, Hindenburg found it personally very difficult forcing the Kaiser to abdicate – but the removal of Wilhelm II was Germany's price for peace. Retiring for a second time in 1919, Hindenburg was again prised back when he was persuaded to accept the presidency of the Weimar Republic – following the death of Ebert, the Republic's inaugural president, in 1925. In July 1932, still convinced that Germany would be better served by a monarch, and still wanting to retire, Hindenburg was again persuaded to stand for re-election as the only alternative to the rising popularity of the Nazi Party. Hindenburg narrowly won the election but a second election, in November 1932, forced Hindenburg into forming a coalition government with Adolf Hitler as his Chancellor.

Following the Reichstag fire in February 1933, Hitler manipulated Hindenburg into suspending the constitution. Hindenburg, increasingly senile, died in 1934. He was buried at Tannenberg, the scene of his greatest triumph, until 1946, when his body was re-interred in the town of Marburg.

Erich Ludendorff 1865–1937

Ludendorff made his reputation early in the war with the capture of the Belgian fortress city, Liège, and, alongside Hindenburg, his successes on the Eastern Front. Following Falkenhayn's dismissal in August 1916, Ludendorff had increasing influence on how Germany was run, both militarily and domestically, gearing the whole German economy up for war. Ludendorff gave his permission for Lenin to return to Russia through Germany, believing, correctly, that Lenin's presence in Petrograd would derail Russia's war effort.

With Russia out of the war, Ludendorff spearheaded Germany's Spring Offensive of 1918, determined to strike before the arrival of American troops. His initial successes were pushed back by the Allies' counter-attack, forcing Ludendorff to canvass US president, Woodrow Wilson, for a mediated peace. On the day of the Armistice, Ludendorff escaped to Sweden, disguised with spectacles and a false beard.

Ludendorff was instrumental in peddling the 'stab in the back' myth, blaming the politicians for Germany's defeat. Vehemently opposed to the Weimar Republic, Ludendorff took part in the failed Kapp putsch of 1920, and Hitler's Munich putsch three years later. Tried for his role in Munich, Ludendorff was acquitted.

In 1924, Ludendorff took a seat in the Reichstag representing the Nazi Party. In 1925, he stood for president against his old ally, Hindenburg, but fared poorly. Keeping his seat in the Reichstag but increasingly senile and disapproving of Hitler, he became an embarrassment to the Nazis, and in 1928 obligingly retired.

Woodrow Wilson 1856–1924

Born in Virginia to a slave-owning Presbyterian minister, Woodrow Wilson became the first Southern US president since Andrew Johnson in 1869. He was elected the twenty-eighth US president in 1911. Wilson, a Democrat, was determined to maintain American neutrality during the war. He was re-elected in 1916 with the slogan 'He kept us out of the war'. Germany's policy of unrestricted submarine warfare, which cost American lives, together with the exposure of the Zimmermann Telegram, forced the President's hand. In April 1917, he sought Congress's mandate to declare war on Germany, a course necessary to make the 'world safe for democracy'.

In January 1918, Wilson, in another address to Congress, introduced his Fourteen Points, a blueprint for a post-war peace that would avoid overly punitive terms for a vanquished Germany and her allies. The establishment of a body to act as an international arbitrator, the League of Nations, was also core to Wilson's philosophy.

By the time the Paris Peace Conference finished in January 1920, not much of the Fourteen Points remained and the terms imposed on Germany in the Treaty of Versailles were indeed punitive. The League of Nations however did become a reality, its inaugural assembly taking place on the last day of the conference. However, there was no representation from the US.

Despite receiving the Nobel Peace Prize in 1919, Wilson returned to America to find much opposition to the treaty both from isolationists and Republicans. While touring the nation, trying to garner support, Wilson suffered the first of several strokes. Paralysed on his left side and blind in one eye, Wilson effectively retired from his duties but remained in office until the election of November 1920.

Wilson's successor in the White House, Republican Warren Harding, neither allowed the US to join the League of Nations nor to ratify the Treaty of Versailles. Wilson died on 3 February 1924, aged sixty-seven.

Edith Cavell 1865–1915

When the Great War broke out, Edith Cavell had been working as a matron in a Brussels nursing school since 1907. Following the German occupation of the city, Cavell hid refugee British soldiers and provided over 200 of them with the means to escape into the neutral Netherlands. Arrested on 3 August 1915, Cavell readily admitted her guilt.

Her case became a *cause célèbre*. The British government, realizing the Germans were acting within their own legality, was unable to intervene. However, the US, as neutrals, pointed to Cavell's nursing credentials and her saving of the lives of German soldiers, as well as British, but to no avail. The nurse was found guilty and sentenced to be shot.

On the evening before her execution, Cavell was visited by an army chaplain. She told him, 'Patriotism is not enough. I must have no hatred or bitterness towards anyone.' The words are inscribed on Cavell's statue, near Trafalgar Square in London.

On 12 October 1915, facing the firing squad, Cavell said, 'My soul, as I believe, is safe, and I am glad to die for my country.' The British made propaganda capital out of the nurse's execution, stoking up anti-German feeling by exploiting the idea of a gentle nurse slaughtered by the German barbarian. The German foreign secretary, Alfred Zimmermann, expressed pity for Cavell but added that she had been 'judged justly'.

Mata Hari 1876–1917

Born to a wealthy Dutch family, Gertrud Margarete Zelle responded to a newspaper advertisement from a Rudolf MacLeod, a Dutch army officer of Scottish descent, seeking a wife. The pair married in 1895 and moved to the Dutch East Indies (Indonesia) where they had two children. Their son died aged two from syphilis, most likely caught from his father – their daughter would die a similar death aged twenty-one. Twenty years older than his wife, MacLeod was an abusive husband and in 1902, on their return to the Netherlands, they separated.

Zelle moved to Paris, where she started to earn a living by modelling and dancing, changing her name to Mata Hari. Exotically dressed, she became a huge success and was feted by the powerful and rich of Paris, taking a number of influential lovers. She travelled numerous times between France and the Netherlands. Her movements and liaisons however caused suspicion.

Arrested by the British, Hari was interrogated. She admitted to passing German information on to the French. In turn, the French discovered evidence, albeit of doubtful authenticity, that she was spying for the Germans. Returning to Paris, Hari was then arrested by the French and accused of being a double agent. The evidence against her was insubstantial, but she was nevertheless found guilty and executed, aged forty-one, on 15 October 1917.

The Unknown Warrior

The vicar of Margate in Kent, the Reverend David Railton, was stationed as a padre on the Western Front when he noticed a temporary grave with the inscription, 'An Unknown British Soldier'. Moved by this simple epitaph, he suggested an idea to the Dean of Westminster, who passed it on to Buckingham Palace. The idea of a tomb of the Unknown Soldier was well received and given the go-ahead.

On 9 November 1920, the remains of six unidentified British soldiers were exhumed – one each from six different battlefields (Aisne, Arras, Cambrai, Marne, Somme, and Ypres). The six corpses were transported to a chapel near Ypres, where they were each covered by the Union flag. There, in the company of a padre (not Reverend Railton), a blindfolded officer entered the chapel and touched one of the bodies.

Placed in a coffin, the chosen soldier was taken to Boulogne, and from there across the Channel on board the HMS *Verdun* (named after the French battle). A train transported it to London. All along the way, the body was afforded pomp and ceremony – processions, gun salutes and, at Boulogne, a salute from Marshal Foch.

Large, silent crowds had assembled to witness the six-horse procession wind its way to The Mall, where the King had unveiled the newly erected Cenotaph. The King and his entourage then followed the cortège to Westminster Abbey where, waiting, was a guard of honour consisting of 100 holders of the Victoria Cross and 100 women who had lost both their husbands and sons during the war.

After a brief service, the coffin was lowered into the grave, 'amongst the kings', and sprinkled with earth brought back from the Western Front. It was covered with a stone slab with the simple inscription, 'An Unknown Soldier'. The following year, the stone was replaced by a slab of Belgian marble and fully inscribed in capitals with text composed by the Dean of Westminster:

BENEATH THIS STONE RESTS THE BODY
OF A BRITISH WARRIOR
UNKNOWN BY NAME OR RANK
BROUGHT FROM FRANCE TO LIE AMONG
THE MOST ILLUSTRIOUS OF THE LAND
AND BURIED HERE ON ARMISTICE DAY
11 NOV 1920, IN THE PRESENCE OF
HIS MAJESTY KING GEORGE V
HIS MINISTERS OF STATE
THE CHIEFS OF HIS FORCES
AND A VAST CONCOURSE OF THE NATION

THUS ARE COMMEMORATED THE MANY
MULTITUDES WHO DURING THE GREAT
WAR OF 1914–1918 GAVE THE MOST THAT
MAN CAN GIVE LIFE ITSELF
FOR GOD
FOR KING AND COUNTRY
FOR LOVED ONES HOME AND EMPIRE
FOR THE SACRED CAUSE OF JUSTICE AND
THE FREEDOM OF THE WORLD

THEY BURIED HIM AMONG THE KINGS BECAUSE HE
HAD DONE GOOD TOWARD GOD AND TOWARD
HIS HOUSE

Appendix Two:
Timeline of World War One

1914

28 June: Archduke Franz Ferdinand, heir to Austria-Hungary's throne, and his wife, Sophie, are assassinated by Serbian nationalist Gavrilo Princip in Sarajevo

28 July: Austrian-Hungarian empire declares war on Serbia

1 August: Germany declares war on Russia

3 August: Germany declares war on France

4 August: Germany invades Luxembourg and Belgium; Great Britain declares war on Germany

6 August: Austrian-Hungarian empire declares war on Russia; Serbia declares war on Germany

7 August: Germans capture Belgian town of Liège; Lord Kitchener calls for volunteers to join the British army

23 August: Battle of Mons begins; Japan declares war on Germany

26 August: The Battle of Tannenberg begins; German colony of Togoland falls to the Allies

29 August: German colony of Samoa falls to New Zealand forces

5–10 September: The First Battle of the Marne begins. Trench warfare established as soldiers on both sides dig in

9–14 September: Battle of the Masurian Lakes

21 September: German New Guinea falls to the Australians

23 September: Japanese siege of German-held Tsingtao begins

19 October: First Battle of Ypres begins

29 October: Turkey enters war on the side of the Central Powers

1 November: Russia declares war on the Ottoman Empire
7 November: Japanese forces capture Tsingtao
21 November: Anglo-Indian invasion of Mesopotamia
24–25 December: Unofficial Christmas truce on the Western Front

1915

19 January: First German zeppelin raid on Great Britain
19 February: The Dardanelles Campaign begins
10–13 March: Battle of Neuve Chapelle
22 April: The Second Battle of Ypres begins. First use of poison gas
24 April: Alleged start of the Armenian Genocide
25 April: Battle of Gallipoli begins
7 May: The British ocean liner RMS *Lusitania* is sunk by a German U-boat
8 May: Nicaragua declares war on Germany
23 May: Italy enters war on the side of the Allies
25 May: British prime minister, Herbert Asquith, forms a coalition government
31 May: First German zeppelin raid on London
9 July: German surrender in South West Africa
6 August: New Allied offensive in Gallipoli from Sulva Bay
5 September: Tsar Nicholas II takes personal command of Russia's armies
25 September: British and Commonwealth forces capture Kut in Mesopotamia; Battle of Loos begins
6 October: Central Powers, including Bulgaria, invade Serbia
9 October: An Allied force lands at Salonika in Greece
12 October: British nurse, Edith Cavell, is executed
14 October: Bulgaria declares war on Serbia
15 October: Belgrade falls to the Austrian-Hungarians
27 November: Defeated Serbian army evacuated to Corfu

7 December: Siege of Kut begins
19 December: Sir Douglas Haig replaces Sir John French as British commander-in-chief

1916
8–9 January: British and Commonwealth forces evacuate Gallipoli
27 January: Britain introduces conscription
21 February: Battle of Verdun begins
9 March: Germany declares war on Portugal
24 April: Easter Uprising in Ireland
29 April: The British surrender at Kut, finishing a 147-day siege
16 May: Sykes–Picot Agreement proposes post-war division of Ottoman territory
31 May: The Battle of Jutland begins
4 June: The Russian Brusilov Offensive begins
5 June: Death of Lord Kitchener by drowning
18 June: Last German forces in Cameroon surrender
1 July: The Battle of the Somme begins
27 August: Romania enters the war on the Allies' side
29 August: Erich von Falkenhayn is replaced as Chief of Staff by Hindenburg and Ludendorff
15 September: The British introduce the tank during the Battle of the Somme
18 November: End of the Battle of the Somme
7 December: David Lloyd George replaces Herbert Asquith as British prime minister
12 December: Richard Nivelle appointed commander-in-chief of French forces

1917
19 January: Britain intercepts and deciphers German secret Zimmermann Telegram sent to Mexico

31 January: Germany announces unrestricted submarine warfare

24 February: British forces recapture Kut

8 March: First Russian Revolution

11 March: British enter Baghdad

15 March: Russian Tsar, Nicholas II, abdicates

6 April: United States declares war on Germany

9 April: Start of the Nivelle Offensive; Battle of Vimy Ridge begins

5 May: Philippe Pétain replaces Nivelle as French commander-in-chief

27 May: Beginning of the French Mutiny

7 June: British capture the Messines Ridge

25 June: First US troops arrive in France

1 July: Beginning of the Kerensky Offensive

17 July: British Royal Family changes name from Saxe-Coburg-Gotha to Windsor

31 July: Third Battle of Ypres (also known as Passchendaele) begins

3 September: German forces capture Riga

15 October: Execution of Mata Hari

24 October: Austrian-Hungarians defeat Italians at the Battle of Caporetto

2 November: Balfour Declaration proposes settlement of Jews within Palestine

7 November: The Bolsheviks overthrow the Russian provisional government

19 November: Clemenceau appointed French prime minister

20 November: Battle of Cambrai

11 December: British capture Jerusalem

16 December: Russia and Germany sign armistice

1918

8 January: US President, Woodrow Wilson, presents his Fourteen Points

3 March: Russia and Germany sign the Treaty of Brest-Litovsk

21 March: Germany launches the Spring Offensive

26 March: French general, Ferdinand Foch, is elevated to 'Allied Supreme Commander of the Western Front'

1 April: Royal Air Force is founded

12 April: Haig issues his 'Backs to the Wall' directive

21 April: German flying ace, Baron Manfred von Richthofen (the Red Baron), is shot down and killed

1 June: Battle of Belleau Wood begins

15 June: Italians halt Austrians at the Battle of River Piave

15 July: The Second Battle of the Marne begins

17 July: Tsar Nicholas II and family are executed

8 August: Start of the Allies' Hundred Days Offensive

27 September: British breach the Hindenburg Line

29 September: Bulgaria surrenders

1 October: British capture Damascus

3 October: Prince Maximilian of Baden appointed Chancellor of Germany

24 October: Austrian-Hungarian army destroyed by Italians at the Battle of Vittorio Veneto

26 October: Ludendorff dismissed

28 October: Czechoslovakia declares independence from the Habsburg Empire

29 October: Kiel mutiny; foundation of the Kingdom of Serbs, Croats and Slovenes, renamed Yugoslavia in 1929

30 October: Turkey signs armistice

31 October Hungary declares independence from the Habsburg Empire

3 November: Austria and Italy sign armistice

9 November: German Kaiser, Wilhelm II, abdicates and flees Germany

11 November: Germany signs armistice. Fighting ceases at 11 a.m.

1919
18 January: Paris Peace Conference opens
6 February: Weimar Republic founded
28 June: The Treaty of Versailles officially ends the First World War

Got Another Hour?

History in an Hour is a series of eBooks to help the reader learn the basic facts of a given subject area. Everything you need to know is presented in a straightforward narrative and in chronological order. No embedded links to divert your attention, nor a daunting book of 600 pages with a 35-page introduction. Just straight in, to the point, sixty minutes, done. Then, having absorbed the basics, you may feel inspired to explore further. Give yourself sixty minutes and see what you can learn…

To find out more visit http://historyinanhour.com or follow us on twitter: http://twitter.com/historyinanhour

1066: History in an Hour by Kaye Jones

Covering the major events of the year 1066, this is a clear account of England's political turmoil during which the country had three different kings and fought three large-scale battles in defence of the kingdom, including the infamous Battle of Hastings.

The Afghan Wars: History in an Hour by Rupert Colley

A comprehensive overview of the wars that have been fought in Afghanistan for almost four decades, including the politics of the Taliban, why Osama Bin Laden was so significant, and why it is still so hard to achieve peace in the country.

The American Civil War: History in an Hour by Kat Smutz

A clear account of the politics and major turning points of the war that split the country in half as the northern and southern states fought over the right to keep slaves, changing American culture forever.

American Slavery: History in an Hour by Kat Smutz

A broad overview of the major events in the history of American slavery, detailing the arrival of the first slaves, the Southern plantations, the Civil War, and the historical and cultural legacy of slavery in the United States.

Ancient Egypt: History in an Hour by Anthony Holmes

A succinct exploration of the historic rise of Egyptian civilisation and its influence on the world, covering Egyptian gods, mummification and burial rituals, and the Pyramids of Giza.

Black History: History in an Hour by Rupert Colley

A clear overview of the long and varied history of African Americans, including everything from slavery, the Civil War and emancipation to the civil rights movement and the Black Panther Party.

The Cold War: History in an Hour by Rupert Colley

A succinct overview of the politics of the non-violent war, from the end of World War II to the collapse of the USSR in 1991, as Russia and America eyed each other with suspicion and hostility.

Dickens: History in an Hour by Kaye Jones

A comprehensive overview of the life of arguably Britain's most successful and beloved writer, including the poverty of his childhood, the evolution of his novels, his tours of Europe and America, and his occasionally scandalous private life.

George Washington: History in an Hour by David B. McCoy

The essential chronicle of George Washington's life, from his middle-class Virginian upbringing to his unanimous election as America's first president, and the prominent role he played in shaping America as we know it today.

The Gunpowder Plot: History in an Hour by Sinead Fitzgibbon

An engaging account of the infamous plot by a group of Catholic traitors, led by Guy Fawkes, to blow up the Houses of Parliament and James I, including details of the motives behind their drastic actions and how the plot came to be discovered.

Henry VIII's Wives: History in an Hour by Julie Wheeler

An inclusive introduction to the six diverse personalities of Henry VIII's wives, the events that led them to their individual fates, and the different impacts they each had on King and country.

Hitler: History in an Hour by Rupert Colley

A coherent overview of Hitler's early life, service in World War I, rise to the top of the Nazi Party and eventually the head of state, covering all the key moments of the dictator's life through to his death and the crumbling of his empire.

JFK: History in an Hour by Sinead Fitzgibbon

A comprehensive insight into the life of America's youngest elected president, assassinated barely one thousand days into his presidency, examining his navigation of the Space Race, his sympathies with the civil rights movement, and the chronic illness that affected him throughout his life.

The Medieval Anarchy: History in an Hour by Kaye Jones

A look at the unprecedented chaos and disorder that followed the death of King Henry I, leading to England's first, and often forgotten, civil war, as well as an overview of the plots and violence that ensued during this nineteen-year bloody conflict.

Nazi Germany: History in an Hour by Rupert Colley

A concise explanation which covers the major events behind the Nazi Party's climb to power, what it was like to live in Nazi Germany, and how Hitler brought the world into war.

The Queen: History in an Hour by Sinead Fitzgibbon

A compelling history of the UK's second-longest-reigning monarch, covering her 1953 coronation to her Diamond Jubilee in 2012 and examining her long reign, during which the British Empire has transformed.

The Reformation: History in an Hour by Edward A. Gosselin

A concise look at the spread of religious dissidence across Europe in the sixteenth century, including the events that caused people to question the ideas of the established Catholic Church and the resulting wars, migration and disunity.

The Russian Revolution: History in an Hour by Rupert Colley

Covering all the major events in a straightforward overview of the greatest political experiment ever conducted, and how it continues to influence both Eastern and Western politics today.

The Siege of Leningrad: History in an Hour by Rupert Colley

A broad account of one of the longest sieges in history in which over the course of 900 days the city of Leningrad resisted German invasion, contributing to the defeat of the Nazis at the cost of over one million civilian lives.

South Africa: History in an Hour by Anthony Holmes

A fascinating overview of South Africa's history of oppression and racial inequality and how after years of violence and apartheid, Nelson Mandela, the country's first black President, led the country to unite and become the 'Rainbow Nation'.

Stalin: History in an Hour by Rupert Colley

A succinct exploration of Joseph Stalin's long leadership of the Soviet Union, covering his rise to power, his role in the Russian Revolution, and his terrifying regime that directly and negatively affected the lives of so many.

Titanic: History in an Hour by Sinead Fitzgibbon

An account of the catastrophe, including the failures of the White Star Line, the significance of class and the legacy of the disaster in Britain and America.

The Vietnam War: History in an Hour by Neil Smith

A clear account of the key events of the most important Cold War-era conflict, including the circumstances leading up to the Vietnam War, the deadly guerrilla warfare, the fall of Saigon and the backlash of anti-war protests in America.

World War Two: History in an Hour by Rupert Colley

Covering the major events in a broad overview of the politics and violence of the most devastating conflict the world has ever seen, and how it changed the world in unimaginable ways.